RACE CAR LEGENDS

The Allisons

Mario Andretti

Dale Earnhardt

A. J. Foyt

Richard Petty

The Unsers

CHELSEA HOUSE PUBLISHERS

RACE CAR LEGENDS

DALE EARNHARDT

Michael Benson

CHELSEA HOUSE PUBLISHERS

New York   Philadelphia

ACKNOWLEDGMENTS
The author wishes to acknowledge the following persons and organiza-
tions, without whose help the creation of this book would have been
impossible: Barry Altmark, Lisa and Tekla Benson, Paul Cockerham,
Norman Jacobs, Katharine Repole, the Mid Manhattan Library, NASCAR,
Milburn Smith and Jose Soto.

Produced by Daniel Bial and Associates
New York, New York

Picture research by Alan Gottlieb
Cover illustration by Neil Machlachlan

3 5 7 9 8 6 4 2

Library of Congress Cataloging-in-Publication Data

Benson, Michael.
        Dale Earnhardt / Michael Benson.
            p.   cm. — (Race car legends)
        Includes bibliographical references and index.
        ISBN 0-7910-3180-2 (hc). — ISBN 0-7910-3181-0 (pbk.)
        1. Earnhardt, Dale, 1951-   —Juvenile literature. 2. Automobile
    racing drivers—United States—Biography—Juvenile literature.
    3. Stock car racing—United States—Juvenile literature.
    [1. Earnhardt, Dale. 2. Automobile racing drivers.] I. Title.
    II. Series.
    GV1032.E18B45 1995
    796.7'2'092—dc20
                                                            [B]95-18224
                                                                 CIP
                                                                  AC

CONTENTS

TO BE A RACE CAR DRIVER

What's the most popular spectator sport in the United States? It's not baseball, football, or basketball. It's not even horse racing (although that's second). America's favorite sport is automobile racing.

To the outsider, it looks simple. You get in your car, keep the accelerator depressed as you hurtle around the track, expect your crew to keep the car in perfect condition, and try not to go deaf as you weave your machine through traffic towards the checkered flag. But in actuality, it's not at all easy. Just as baseball isn't just hit the ball with the bat and run around the bases, so racing is full of subtleties that might not immediately attract the eye.

What does it take to be a world-class race car driver? The more you know about the lives of the greats, the more it becomes clear that each successful driver is also an extraordinary person in many ways. Each is an athlete, gifted with unusual vision, coordination, and the will to win. The concentration necessary to send a car hurtling around a track at 200 miles per hour for hour after hour, when a momentary lapse can cause instant death for you and any unfortunate driver near you, is phenomenal. Any driver worth his salt must be strong, self-confident, resilient, willing to take risks in order to have an opportunity to win.

In addition, the top drivers all have to be good businessmen and know how to put together a winning team. They have to find sponsors to put them in competitive cars. They rely on a pit crew to make sure that their car always is in peak performance condition. And they have to be mentally prepared each race day to take into consideration a host of factors: weather, the other racers, the condition of the track, and how the car is responding on that day. Without everything right, a driver won't stand a chance of winning.

All the drivers in this series grew up around race cars. The fathers of Richard Petty and Dale Earnhardt were very successful race car drivers themselves. A. J. Foyt's father was a part-time racer and a full-time mechanic; the Allisons and Unsers are an extended family of racers. Only Mario Andretti's father disapproved of his son's racing. Yet Mario and his twin brother Aldo devoted themselves to racing at a young age; today, the Andretti family boasts three stand-out racers in Mario and Aldo's sons.

Yet despite the knowledge and connections a family can provide, few of the legendary racers portrayed in this series met with immediate success. They needed to prove themselves in sprint cars or midget cars before they were allowed to get behind the wheel of a contending stock car or a phenomenally expensive Indy car. They needed to be tested in the tough races on the hardscrabble tracks before they learned enough to handle the race situations at Daytona or the Brickyard. They needed to learn how to get the most out of whatever vehicle they were piloting, including knowing how to fix an engine in the wee hours of the night before a big race.

Virtually every driver has also had to learn to face adversity. Crashes often take the lives of friends or relatives. Every driver has been lucky at one point or another to survive a scare or a bad accident. The mother of Al and Bobby Unser said it best, though, when she remarked, "We've had our tragedies, but what family hasn't? I don't blame racing. I love racing as our whole family has...Racing is this family's life and no one ever had a closer family."

What each driver has proved is that success in this most grueling sport takes commitment. Walter Payton, the great football running back, and Paul Newman, star of many blockbuster movies, have both taken up racing—and proved they have some talent behind the wheel. Still, it's evident that neither has been able to provide the devotion it takes in order to be successful at the highest levels.

A FULL-FLEDGED LEGEND

It is October 23, 1994, and Dale Earnhardt, in his black Chevrolet Lumina, is leading the AC-Delco 500 stock car race on the North Carolina Speedway in Rockingham. The race is important to Earnhardt because he is about to win the National Association of Stock Car Auto Racing (NASCAR) driving championship—he hopes. Only one man is in contention: Rusty Wallace, who had won a driving championship himself in 1989. If Earnhardt can finish third, regardless of what Wallace does, he'll wrap up his seventh championship, and it will tie him with the legendary Richard Petty for the most championships won by any driver.

The first word most experts use when describing Dale Earnhardt's racing style is "aggressive." If that word were used to describe any other driver, chances are that it would not be intended as a compliment, but Dale has the

In 1994, Dale Earnhardt made history by winning his seventh driving championship. Wherever he and his famous black number 3 Chevrolet Lumina go, they inspire fear and awe in other drivers.

9

Off the racetrack, Earnhardt can be friendly and down to earth. On the racetrack, there's no one with greater competitive fire.

instincts and the skills to be aggressive without being reckless.

Earnhardt strikes fear into the hearts of other drivers. He shows up like a big "Danger" sign in a driver's rear-view mirror. The driver knows he has to cope with Dale's arsenal of short-track moves. Then Dale is right on his bumper.

Next thing you know, the driver has lost his concentration just long enough to let Earnhardt shoot by. Sometimes a competitor will be so rattled by Earnhardt's relentless charging that he will spin out of control completely.

Earnhardt's real virtue on the race track is confidence. His faith in his own driving ability is such that he can quickly figure out the limits of a car's performance, and his touch is so deft that he can take a car beyond those limits for long periods when he needs to.

Getting through traffic is a skill that Dale had to learn if he wanted to win. Why? Well, the truth of the matter is that Dale has never been the world's greatest qualifier. The black number 3 car often starts towards the middle or the back of the pack—in Rockingham he started 20th on the starting grid—but it usually isn't long before Earnhardt starts charging through the field.

Earnhardt has the knack of finishing races, even the races he doesn't win. That's a good skill to have because the Winston Cup points system rewards endurance. Of course, winning is always the goal, but you also have to have a car that's not going to break down. You have to avoid trouble on the track.

Whenever trouble breaks out on the track, Dale is a ninja. There is a mystical quality to his rides. When his competitors look in the rear-view mirror, there he is. When the checkered flag comes out, there he is. When there's trouble, he's always somewhere else, out of harm's way. He takes risks, certainly, but always knows when a risk is worth taking.

Dale tries to explain his uncanny skill. "I guess I learned that on the Winston Racing Series (short) tracks. If something happens in front of you there, you had better be able to make a decision in a tenth of a second or you are going to be in the middle of it, too," he says.

"That's something that has been carried over throughout my career. It's part of experience, part of learning. As more and more guys come into NASCAR Winston Cup from the Winston Racing Series, you are seeing more and more guys with that same kind of instinct."

The 1994 season started as one of disappointment and sorrow for Dale Earnhardt. The first race of the year is the Daytona 500, the biggest and most important event in stock-car racing. Somehow, Dale has never won this event at the Daytona International Speedway, in Daytona, Florida.

"I've lost every way you can imagine. I shouldn't say that. I'll probably come up with a new one," Dales says with a laugh.

But Dale wasn't going to get much enjoyment out of the 1994 Speedweek, no matter how well he performed on the track. That's because Dale's "huntin' and fishin' buddy," Neil Bonnett, crashed on February 11, 1994. In a practice run, Bonnett's Chevy Lumina hit the outside wall head-on coming out of Turn 4. He did not survive.

Bonnett had been known for years for the way he could come back again and again from the hard times. He had suffered a broken sternum in 1989, but he'd come back. In 1990, at Darlington, in only the fifth race of the season, Bonnett's Number 21 Citgo Ford Thunderbird was involved in a multi-car wreck on the main straightaway that left him with serious head injuries, and what developed into a recurring case of memory loss. Winston Cup fans understood the sad irony that his death came in the midst of another comeback.

Doctors had advised Bonnett to hang up his helmet. It wasn't long before he was hired to call races on television. His easy-going nature made him a hit with viewers, and he was a familiar sight in the garage area on race day with his navy blazer and headphones.

But being out of the driver's seat ate away at the soul of a man who'd won 18 Winston Cup races, as well as nearly $4 million in prize money. Neil kept involved by helping out his son, David, launch a Busch Grand National career, but it wasn't really enough for Bonnett.

Nobody knew this better than Dale. In May 1993, Earnhardt offered Bonnett a chance to do some test driving for Richard Childress Racing. The six-time Winston Cup champion was looking for advice from Bonnett, while at the same time offering him a no-pressure scenario to get some seat time. A week later, Bonnett received medical clearance to race again.

Rookie Rodney Orr was also killed in a crash during that horrible week in Daytona. Thus, on

race day, it was unusually somber at the Florida track. But Dale knew that the paying customers were the boss, and grief aside, the show must go on.

Everyone who qualified for the races showed up and took the green flag.

Much has been said over the years about Dale's Daytona jinx. Well, let's make one thing clear. Dale Earnhardt isn't snakebit at Daytona, only in the Daytona 500.

In all the other races he chooses to compete in at Daytona, he excels, just as he does at most other Winston Cup tracks. So it wasn't any

Earnhardt, on the outside track, passing slower cars at the 1994 Goody's 300. He went on to victory in this race—the fifth consecutive time he had won it.

shock when Earnhardt won the 300-mile opening race in the Busch Grand National series on February 19, 1994.

It was his fifth consecutive victory in this race.

There was an 11-car accident on the sixth lap when Mike Garvey spun, starting a chain reaction. Mike Stefanik was the most seriously injured; he broke bones in his right big toe and left ankle.

Naturally, Dale was nowhere around at the time of the accident.

On Lap 116, Earnhardt, in his usual black Chevy Lumina, was in fourth place, behind Terry Labonte, Bill Elliott, and race-leader Ernie Irvan. Elliott went down with engine trouble with less than 10 miles to go in the race.

Soon thereafter Labonte passed Irvan, and— because of a vacuum created by tailgating at high speeds, called drafting—Labonte pulled Earnhardt with him as they passed Irvan.

For most of the last lap (Lap 120) Earnhardt remained on Labonte's rear bumper, preparing for his move. Labonte tried as hard as he could, weaving on the track, to keep Earnhardt behind him.

But Dale would not be denied. On the third-to-last turn, he found an opening on the inside, and went for the pass. Dale Jarrett in a Lumina and Chad Little in a Thunderbird followed in Earnhardt's wake and passed Labonte as well.

Jarrett then tried to slingshot past Earnhardt, but Dale held on to win by half a car length. Jarrett was second, Little third, and Labonte fourth. Earnhardt took home a nifty $50,933 for his victory.

The next day brought the Daytona 500, and

again—as seems to happen every year—Dale's luck ran out. He was leading the race with 50 miles left when he ran into car trouble. His wheels weren't responding to the steering wheel properly and the car wouldn't handle right. The Earnhardt Daytona jinx had struck again.

All of a sudden, Earnhardt was pushed up high on a turn and started to battle his steering wheel as if he were driving on a quarter-mile dirt track. Ernie Irvan, who had been in contention, also ran into car problems and dropped back suddenly. Sterling Marlin moved into the lead to stay.

There were brighter days in 1994 to come. Dale's biggest win of the season came at the Talladega Superspeedway in Talladega, Alabama, on May 1, in the Winston Select 500.

Jimmy Spencer, Sterling Marlin, Ernie Irvan, and Dale were battling at the front with ten laps left to go. With three laps to the checkered flag, Michael Waltrip pushed his nose into the picture.

Earnhardt was still in front, Michael Waltrip second, Ken Schrader moved into third, and Irvan into fourth. On the last lap, it was Earnhardt and Irvan in a dogfight to the finish. Earnhardt brought home his 62nd Winston Cup victory by less than a car length. For Dale, who had turned 43 the previous Friday, this win at Talladega was a belated birthday present.

With the season winding down, Earnhardt had showed again why he's the best driver on the circuit. All he needed to do was finish third at the AC-Delco 500 to wrap up his seventh Winston Cup championship. On many days, Rusty Wallace can give Earnhardt a run for his money. But Wallace, the other driver on the

Car number 3 takes the inside and powers on to victory at the 1994 Winston Select 500.

Winston Cup circuit who drives a black car—the number 2 Miller Genuine Draft Ford Thunderbird—experienced engine failure with 192 laps left in the race. That was good enough only for a 35th-place finish.

The crowd let out a collective moan when Rusty called it a day. Both drivers wanted the championship to be decided on the track rather than "behind the wall" in the garage area.

Even with the title now decided, Earnhardt felt no need to let up.

When the flag man waved the white flag, letting the drivers know that there was only one lap left in the race, it was Earnhardt crossing the start-finish line in first.

Right on Dale's tail was Rick Mast in a Ford Thunderbird. Though Dale had been ahead for the last 76 laps, Mast had been steadily gaining on him. Could he pass Dale with only one lap to go?

Folks who've driven on the Winston Cup circuit, the major leagues of stock car racing, will tell you that passing Dale Earnhardt during the last laps of a race is next to impossible.

So it didn't really shock anyone when Mast tried to pass several times during that last lap, only to be cut off with ease by Dale. When the checkered flag waved, showing that the race is over, Dale was still ahead—even if only by one and a half car lengths.

The official margin of victory was .06 seconds. It takes about ten times longer than that to blink. Dale's average speed for the race was 126.407 mph (miles per hour).

Dale's earnings for the AC-Delco victory were $60,600—but this was not the biggest prize of Dale's day.

In winning the new championship, Dale had accomplished something that folks once thought impossible. The 6'1", 185-pounder had just won his seventh Winston Cup crown, tying the record set by "The King" himself, Richard Petty. They thought it couldn't be done—certainly not this soon. That's like Henry Aaron tying Babe Ruth's home run record, or a football player tying Jerry Rice's record for career touchdowns.

Now Dale is a legend, a full-fledged legend, whether he likes it or not. His career record reads: 480 starts, 63 wins, 217 top fives, and 314 top tens.

Although Dale's victory in North Carolina was only his first in his last 19 races, he remains in sixth place on the all-time Winston Cup winners list, behind only Cale Yarborough, Darrell Waltrip, Bobby Allison, David Pearson and Richard Petty.

Dale remains the only stock car driver to win more than $3 million in a year, and he has done it three times.

"I never thought I'd see one [championship]," Dale says. "You really grow up in racing, running around with your dad and your dad is your idol and everything revolves around him. You just want to race and you finally get your opportunity..."

Dale's voice trails off. Maybe it hasn't quite sunk in. Maybe it all has happened too fast. His seven championships have come in just 15 full Winston Cup seasons. Petty drove the circuit for 35 years!

He's gone from the young rowdy one who needed a haircut and made folks on pit road nervous to a man who can now stand on the same plateau as Richard Petty and he has done it with a driving skill and style the likes of which stock car racing may never see again.

After winning the 1994 championship in Rockingham, Dale remembered Neil Bonnett. "Neil was my best buddy, and I want to dedicate this championship to him. He was the greatest I've ever known."

Although seven Winston Cup championships are now his, Earnhardt shows no signs of being through. "People say I'm from the old school. They say, 'He races harder than he should sometimes.' But I learned from the guys who raced like that.

"As a boy I remember standing on the tailgate of a pickup truck down in Columbia [South Carolina], watching my daddy race against David Pearson, Lee Petty, all of 'em. I come from where they been," Dale says.

His eyes look at something far away for a moment, as the humble star recalls where he comes from.

2

RALPH'S KID

alph Dale Earnhardt was born on April 29, 1952, in Kannapolis, North Carolina. His father, Ralph Earnhardt, was a famous NASCAR dirt-track warrior during the 1950s. In fact, Dale's daddy, Ralph, won the Sportsman title in 1956.

Ralph ran a one-man operation. He built the engine, built the car, and drove in the race. He was one of the few dirt-track drivers from those days who could make more than $100,000 a year without bootlegging on the side.

Touring the local tracks, Ralph would win a race on Thursday night, Friday night, Saturday night, and on Sunday afternoon. Racers from as far away as California came to Kannapolis to ask his advice.

In later years, Ralph had the opportunity to drive regularly on the Grand National circuit, what we call the Winston Cup series today—but

Earnhardt, here accepting his Driver of the Year trophy in 1994, speaks modestly about his achievements. He has always been quick to credit all he learned from his father.

Ralph Earnhardt pushes his Pontiac to the limit at a 1961 race at Daytona. Ned Jarrett—who won the drivers' championship that year—tries to keep pace.

that would have meant working for a boss and Ralph didn't believe in bosses.

Humpy Wheeler, now the president of the Charlotte Motor Speedway, remembers Ralph well from the old days: "Ralph was a very stoic person," Humpy says.

"He was tall, thin and always had a flattop or buzz haircut. At the track he didn't have much to say, and he didn't work on his car when he arrived. When that car came off the trailer, he was ready to race.

"Ralph's style was interesting, because of what he would do. He would usually run second and put constant pressure on the frontrunner, be inches away from him, particularly at tracks that were really hard to drive, like Columbia Speedway.

"Ralph would never have said this to anyone, of course, but the great drivers are like the great poker players: They don't always show their hand.

"In other words, maybe Ralph could have lapped the field, but if he'd done that, NASCAR would have been all over him, trying to figure out what he had in his car that nobody else had."

In later years, every word Humpy said of Ralph could be used to describe Dale.

Many top racers have learned the love of the sport from their families. Richard Petty's father was an outstanding driver—Lee Petty won back-to-back drivers championships in 1958 and 1959. The brothers Bobby and Donnie Allison each had children who became competitive drivers; Davey Allison, Bobby's son, was on his way to becoming one of the best and most popular drivers of all time when he died in a tragic helicopter accident.

A. J. Foyt's father did not do much driving, but like Ralph Earnhardt, he was a standout mechanic. Tony Foyt taught A. J. all he needed to know so that he could get the most out of every car he piloted.

This is not to say that all parents are happy to see their sons go into racing. Lee Petty made Richard work in his garage for three years before loaning him a car and letting him enter a race.

Ralph Earnhardt too did not encourage Dale to become a race-car driver. In fact, Dale defied his daddy when, at age 15, he dropped out of high school and went into the racing trade. It took him four years before he got his chance out on the track, but once he got his opportunity, he made the most of it. During the early years of Dale's career, the younger Earnhardt would sometimes blow the field away in a race, lapping the pack early and often. This ticked Ralph off.

Ralph would take his young son aside and say, "Never pull away and leave them too far behind. Pass the guy on the last lap and win the race—and always let the fans believe that the second-place guy can beat you."

Jeff Hammond, who worked at the Charlotte Motor Speedway in the early 1970s, remembers Ralph from the latter part of his career: "Ralph was the kind of driver, if you raced him clean, he'd race you clean. But if you lay on him or beat on him, you better be prepared for one wild ride.

"He always expected fair treatment, but if someone did him wrong, he'd make darn sure he paid him back double. And it's how he taught Dale to race."

After several years working odd jobs at the race tracks, Dale finally began his professional auto-racing career, touring the small tracks of the Carolinas, in 1971 when he was just 19.

The following year, because of a severe case of hardening of the arteries, Ralph Earnhardt was told by doctors that he could never drive a race car again. Just the fact that Ralph went to the doctor let everyone know how bad he felt, because Ralph neither liked nor trusted doctors.

In 1973, Dale's father, Ralph, died of a massive heart attack at the age of 44. Dale was 20.

It has been said that Dale Earnhardt's take-no-prisoners driving style closely resembles that of his late father Ralph. What is their secret?

"There are no deep, dark secrets," Dale says today. "That's part of the philosophy my daddy taught me: You prepare that race car the best you can, and you work hard and you run hard and you keep your composure about you, and it'll all work out."

"You establish your territory. And you always stay cool on the racetrack," Ralph Earnhardt used to tell Dale—which Dale does, in spades.

3

DALE BECOMES A STAR

Dale's first Winston Cup start came in the 1975 World 600 at the Charlotte Motor Speedway, in Charlotte, North Carolina. He started in 33rd position, and finished 22nd.

Apparently the guy finishing right behind him was the most impressed. That man was Richard Childress, who today is the owner of the GM Goodwrench Racing Team, as well as Earnhardt's friend and boss.

"I knew the first time I saw him drive I wouldn't mind having him drive my car," Childress says today. "But I had never considered being just a car owner at that point. When I finally made that decision back in 1981, it was the toughest decision I had ever made. Looking back, of course, it was also the smartest."

If one tried to pinpoint the one race that

In 1979, Earnhardt's excellent outings won him Rookie of the Year honors—the same year Richard Petty won his seventh driving championship. Here Earnhardt competes at the Daytona 500—the only major race he has yet to win. Dale is in the number 2 car, behind Bobby Allison's number 15 car.

27

made Dale a star, the best pick would be the October 7, 1978, World Service Life 300 at Charlotte. The race was a 28-lead-change classic in what would now be called the Busch Grand National tour, but was then known as the Late Model Sportsman division.

The favorite to win the race was the legendary veteran Bobby Allison, driving an AMC Matador. Dale drove the second car for a two-car Chevy team; the main driver of the team was Dave Marcis.

Darrell Waltrip started on the pole in another Chevrolet, while Harry Gant lined up on the outside of the front row in an Oldsmobile. Allison and Marcis made up the second row.

Dale started on the outside of the fourth row, beside Butch Lindley. Allison took an early lead in the race but relinquished the front-runner spot to Waltrip after six laps.

Waltrip held the lead until Lap 59 when he cut a tire. Marcis pushed into the lead—and Dale was right behind him. Marcis remained out in front for the next 22 laps.

On Lap 84, Dale took the lead for the first time, but he only held onto it for five laps. Then it was Harry Gant's turn to lead the parade. Gant held the lead on and off until past midway in the race, at which time he too cut a tire and was out of the running.

The final 50 laps were an Allison-Earnhardt duel all the way. The Matador led for 11 laps, but Earnhardt came right back to take the point through Lap 159.

Back and forth they went. Again and again and again. The pair traded the lead nine times more before running much of the final 20 laps side by side.

On Lap 197, with three laps to go, Allison passed Earnhardt for the last time, and he ended up beating Dale to the checkered flag by less than a carlength.

The crowd of 42,500 had been standing most of the way. Finally, they fell into their seats exhausted. It was true that Allison had won the race, but everyone had expected that to happen.

All the talk was of that up-and-coming kid, the brash and wild Dale Earnhardt, who had provided them with the most exciting race they had seen in a long while.

"It was a heck of ride," Dale said after the race. "I lost—but how can I be upset? It was a thrill to run like that against these guys."

That might have been the moment that Dale became a star.

Rookies in Winston Cup Racing are usually expected to stay in the slow lane and not get in the leaders' way. But Dale was not the average rookie.

Although he won only one race in 1979, he finished in the top ten in 17 out of 27 races. His record easily captured him Rookie of the Year honors. All the veterans on the Winston Cup tour now had significantly more competition than before.

THE RAGTAG CREW

Nobody gave Dale much of a chance in 1980. From the outside, looking in, the cards seemed to be stacked against him. His crew was terribly young and inexperienced, and, well, some of them didn't seem to have their heads screwed on too tight. A lot of them were from California, and they seemed too laid back, too flaky to be scrambling around a NASCAR pit road.

Dale didn't add much sanity to the team's reputation. Dale was as fun-loving off the track as he was intense on it. Dale had been spotted cruising the garage area at various race tracks in his then blue and yellow Monte Carlo race car, all slouched down in the front seat like the lowest of the low riders.

Dale's prospects for on-track success didn't improve, it appeared, when crew chief Jake Elder—apparently an old fuddy-duddy—desert-

By finishing fifth at the Los Angeles Times 500 in 1980, Earnhardt earned enough points to win his first NASCAR Grand National Championship. The newspaper he's holding here is a dummy copy.

ed the team in the middle of the season.

Many laughed when Elder's replacement turned out to be Doug Richert. Richert, though he'd been a member of the team for four years, even before Dale signed on as driver, was only 20 years old.

But the arrival of Richert turned out to be the best thing that could have happened to Dale's team. Things began to gel and the season turned into a two-man battle for the points championship between Dale and three-time champion Cale Yarborough.

Yarborough's crew chief was a tad older than Dale's. Heading up Yarborough's team was the legendary former driver Junior Johnson.

To many of today's fans, Junior Johnson is stock-car racing. He is a product of the sport's down-and-dirty past. In states where liquor sales were illegal, Junior learned his driving skills keeping his whiskey car a step ahead of federal revenue agents.

He was one of the sport's greatest drivers during the 1950s and early 1960s. Junior won 50 Grand National (now Winston Cup) races in just 13 years. Today, he is one of the circuit's top owners. His drivers have won six Winston Cup championships.

"We had something to prove," recalled Richert. "We were supposed to fall on our butts, go down the tubes. We didn't. There was a lot of adrenaline flowing. We knew we could do the job."

One of Dale's big wins during the stretch run in late September was in the Old Dominion 500 in Martinsville, Virginia. Dale took the lead when Cale Yarborough made a brief, unscheduled pit stop with 12 laps left. He held on for the win despite a late charge by Buddy Baker, who moved up two positions into second place in the last few laps and took the checkered flag only 1.35 seconds behind Dale.

A week later, Earnhardt again finished first in the National 500 at the Charlotte Motor Speedway in Charlotte, North Carolina. The ragtag crew nailed a beauty of a pit stop with 75 laps to go, giving Dale just enough of an advantage for him to beat Cale Yarborough by 1.83 seconds.

Going into the final race of the year, The Los Angeles Times 500 at the 2.5-mile Ontario Motor Speedway in Ontario, California, Dale was ahead of Yarborough by only 29 points.

That meant that even if Yarborough won the race, Earnhardt could still win the championship if he finished fifth or better.

There was no question about who had the faster car. Yarborough had started from the pole a record 13 times during the season. Dale had not started from the pole once.

So why was Dale ahead in points? David Ifft, Benny Parsons' crew chief, had a theory. "I'll tell you what makes that car run. Dale Earnhardt makes that car run. He's been driving like a wild man to make up for a lack of horsepower all year. Been going into the corners deeper and just throwing it the rest of the way around. Thing is, he's good enough to get away with it."

Just hours before he was to qualify for the Ontario race, Dale might have been feeling some nerves—but he sure didn't show it. He stretched out on the floor of his garage, closed his eyes, and sawed some wood.

Yarborough had qualified for the race with a lap at 155.499 mph, good enough for the pole.

In the 1980 Mason-Dixon 500, Dale Earnhardt, in the number 2 car, and Richard Petty, in his famous number-43 car, went nose-to-nose.

Dale didn't care about Yarborough's superior car. As he climbed into his Monte Carlo before qualifying, Dale said, "Cale's car is strong! But damn! I want to run faster than that son of a gun."

To pick up time, Dale drove dangerously deep into Ontario's tough Turn 1 before easing off on the throttle, a full 50 yards deeper than Yarborough had gone.

The result was a qualifying speed of 154.855, not good enough to put him on the pole, but good enough to put him on the front row, right next to Yarborough.

"That's just where I want to be," Dale said, when he learned the results of his qualifying run.

Come race day, Cale and Dale sat side by side on the starting grid.

"Use your head," Yarborough said.

"That goes for both of us," Dale replied.

Just before pulling out, Yarborough flashed Earnhardt a big "may the best man win" thumbs up, which Dale returned wholeheartedly.

That was when things started going bad for Dale. The wind began to whip up with gusts of 30–40 mph, and it blew the Monte Carlo all over the road.

The front pack soon left Earnhardt behind as Dale battled an increasingly troublesome handling problem. Meanwhile, Yarborough stayed up front.

On the 69th lap a yellow flag came out. A yellow flag tells the drivers to slow down and not to pass because there is trouble somewhere on the track. It's a good time to pit ordinarily, but Dale and his crew botched this one good. They miscalculated Dale's position on the track relative to the leader and pitted too soon.

The mistake cost Dale a lap. This led to an exciting stretch where Dale and Cale battled it out side by side, Dale one lap down. Earnhardt tried, and repeatedly failed, to unlap himself.

Worse than being a lap down, Dale had fallen into sixth place—and he needed to finish at least fifth to take home the series championship. (The series, in those days, was known as the Grand National Series. This is the same series that is today known as the Winston Cup Series, and not to be confused with today's secondary Busch Grand National Series.)

Dale's luck turned for a time on Lap 145 when Darrell Waltrip's blown engine brought out a yellow. Since Waltrip had been ahead of Earnhardt, Dale automatically moved up into fifth place.

Sometimes a driver's best friend is another driver's bad luck.

Only six laps after the Waltrip yellow, a second caution came out when a car spun, and it was on this restart that Dale got a jump on the pack to the green flag and unlapped himself.

The next time a yellow flag came out, Earnhardt was legally able to race around the track and catch up with the lead pack. The green flag at Lap 156 again found Dale getting a jump on the pack. This time when he passed Yarborough it was to take the lead.

Cale and Dale exchanged the lead. The two cars put some space between them and the rest of the field. Then it came time for the final pit stops of the race.

Dale couldn't have fouled up the pit stop more if he had tried. It was a rare case of brain fade from a guy known to maintain an even strain.

First he skidded the Monte Carlo into his own pit wall, forcing his crew to scurry for their lives. The crew, however, quickly got it together and the pit stop commenced.

But Dale's fouling up wasn't through. Earnhardt thought he had gotten the sign that his crew was finished and tore out of his pit with a squeal. Unfortunately, one tire was only partially on—and it was the old tire, at that, worn to the cord. The Monte Carlo had still been up on the jack.

A black flag came out, ordering Dale to return to the pits so that the three missing lug nuts could be put on the unchanged tire. This was done efficiently.

Dale's hopes of winning the race were gone, but he managed to pull out of pit road and back onto the track just in time to move into fifth place.

Yarborough finished third, behind winner Benny Parsons and second-place finisher Neil Bonnett. Dale held on to fifth place—and was the NASCAR champ. He had finished the 31-race season with five victories, 19 top five finishes, and 24 top ten finishes. Dale won the points championship by a minuscule five points, and—by the skin of his teeth—became the first champion to win NASCAR's highest honors in only his second year on the circuit.

In the opening years of Earnhardt's career, other drivers hung the nickname "Ironhead" on him. This was half complimentary, half insulting. By calling him "Ironhead," they were saying he had an unusual willingness to take risks and had a stubborn streak in him—and no one knows more about risks and stubbornness than other race-car drivers. But they also recognized that "Ironhead" used these skills to win a lot of races, and soon that nickname gave way to another: "The Terminator."

Use of this nickname showed Earnhardt had won the respect of his competitors. And the nickname fit. Dale knew how to keep his clamps on first place when the checkered flag was upcoming better than anyone else.

5

THE CHILDRESS ERA

In 1981, Richard Childress decided that his days inside a race car were over. He was going to run his race team instead, and went looking for someone to replace him behind the wheel.

In the meantime, it was true that Dale's rag-tag team had won the championship the year before, but Dale didn't realistically expect it to repeat the miracle, and was looking for a more established team to latch onto.

Earnhardt and Childress were made for each other. Along with fulfilling each other's professional needs, they also had a lot in common. Both of them had come up the hard way. They had had to borrow money to get started in the racing business and had paid off their debts with their success.

The partnership lasted only a year in its first attempt. Dale didn't win any races that year, but he finished in the top five nine times and in the

At first turn of the 1982 Pocono 500, Dale Earnhardt and Tim Richmond got into an accident. Earnhardt's car overturned. Here Richmond assists Earnhardt as Dale's leg needed medical attention.

top ten 17 times, in a 31-race season. Earnhardt finished seventh in the running for the points championship.

Dale was getting to the point where he could call his shots, and, by the end of the 1981 season, Richard simply couldn't afford him anymore. Dale left Childress at the end of the season and signed to drive for the legendary race-car owner, Bud Moore. The combination didn't click and Dale failed to finish in the top ten in the Winston Cup points standings in 1982 for the only time in the decade.

Moore and Earnhardt tried it as a team again in 1983, and this time Dale fared better, finishing eighth in the point standings. In 30 races that year, Dale won two, finished in the top five nine times and in the top ten 14 times.

Still, Dale yearned to drive for his buddy Childress again. So, after two years of racing for Bud Moore, Dale returned to Richard Childress Racing, this time to stay.

Six of Dale's seven Winston Cup championships would be for Richard Childress Racing Enterprises. "Richard Childress and I see things on the same wavelength," Dale says today. "I plan on driving for him until I retire."

Dale's first and most spectacular win of the 1984 Winston Cup season came on July 29 in the Talladega 500 in Talladega, Alabama, in front of 94,000 people.

The race was memorable because the victory featured one of Earnhardt's instinctive, genius moves on the track.

With six laps left in the race, Terry Labonte took the lead and appeared to be on his way to victory. There were 15 cars still on the lead lap.

"I knew I had to be in the right place at the

right time. It was one of those races," Dale said later.

When the white flag was waved, indicating one lap left, Labonte was still in the lead—but the Ol' Intimidator was riding right on his tail!

On the backstretch Labonte blinked and Earnhardt shot by. Buddy Baker followed right behind Dale and moved into second.

The Chevy instantly put distance between itself and the other cars. By the time he came down the home stretch, the checkered flag poised and ready, he was confident enough to wave to the crowd.

That was how Dale became the first driver ever to win the Talladega 500 twice in a row. His average speed was 155.585. The victory earned him $47,100. Earnhardt has since won the Talladega 500 twice more. No one else has won it more than two times.

Earnhardt's second (and last, as it turned out) win of the 1984 season came in the Atlanta Journal 500 on November 11 at the Atlanta Motor Speedway. His average speed for that race was 134.610 mph on the 1.5-mile oval.

The prize money for first place was $40,610. Unfortunately, the Atlanta race will always be most remembered for the tragic death of rookie Terry Schoonover who crashed into the wall on the 129th lap.

Earnhardt finished fourth in the points standings on the season, behind winner Terry Labonte, Harry Gant, and Bill Elliott. In 30 races, Dale won twice, had 12 top-fives and finished in the top ten 22 times.

Most drivers would be happy with such results. For Earnhardt, that was just a prelude before he hit his prime.

6

THREE MORE CHAMPIONSHIPS

In 1985, Dale finished a disappointing eighth in the point standings. In 28 races, Dale won four of them, but his consistency was not what it had been in the past—or what it was to become. He had ten top five finishes, but only managed to finish in the top ten 16 times.

On February 23, 1986, during only the second points race of the season, the Miller 400, at the Richmond Fairgrounds Raceway in Richmond, Virginia, Dale disobeyed one of Daddy Ralph's most important rules: Dale lost his cool on the track—and it cost him.

He was leading the race with three laps to go when Darrell Waltrip tried to pass him on the back straightaway. Earnhardt purposefully swerved into Waltrip, causing both cars to crash.

Dale Earnhardt holds up three fingers, celebrating the three victories he had in one week, all at the Daytona International Speedway. On February 9, 1986, he won the Busch Clash. Four days later, he won a 7-Eleven 125-mile qualifying race. And on the 15th, he came in first at the Goody's 300.

Keeping a cool head is a necessary talent among race-car drivers. Here Dale Earnhardt catches 40 winks while waiting for his turn to qualify at the Atlanta Journal 500.

This sent off a chain reaction that damaged several other cars. Both Earnhardt and Waltrip were able to continue, despite some bent sheet metal, and no one was injured in the incident.

Kyle Petty steered his way through the wreckage for the victory and Joe Ruttman finished second. Dale managed to finish third, but he knew he was in trouble.

NASCAR decided to fine Dale $5,000 and put him on probation for the rest of the season. Any more dangerous moves like the one at Richmond and Dale would be banned from future NASCAR races.

Dale did manage to stay out of trouble, but he didn't let the probation slow him down. In fact, in April, Dale won back-to-back races at Darlington and in the First Union 400.

In the North Wilkesboro race, Dale held off a challenge by Ricky Rudd in the late going and won his first race ever on the 5/8-mile track. His average speed was 88.417 mph.

Dale had quite a weekend in Charlotte at the beginning of October 1986. On Saturday, October 4, Dale won the All Pro 300, earning $64,895 in the process, and then won the Winston Cup race on Sunday for an additional $82,050 in prize money. In the Sunday race, Dale beat Harry Gant by 1.9 seconds. The big weekend pushed Dale's earnings for the year over the $1 million mark.

In the final race of the year, the Atlanta

Journal 500, Dale not only won the race and clinched his second Winston Cup championship, but he shattered the track record in the process.

Earnhardt leads the pack at the 1986 Transouth.

The previous fastest race in Atlanta was 144.945 mph set by Benny Parsons in the 1984 Coca Cola 500. Dale blew that away and won the 1986 race with an average speed of 152.523 mph. Second place went to Richard Petty, who was more than a lap behind when Dale finished the race.

Second place in the points championship went to Darrell Waltrip. Waltrip had had a chance to challenge Earnhardt for the championship, but when he was forced to retire with mechanical problems on the 83rd lap, Earnhardt was assured of the victory.

Dale started 29 races, won five of them, finished in the top five 16 times and finished in the top ten 23 times. His winnings for the year were $1,768,880.

Dale won his third Winston Cup championship in 1987, defeating second-place Bill Elliott by a whopping 489 points. In no season has Dale won more races than he did in 1987.

Earnhardt brought home the Winston Cup checkers on 11 different occasions in 1987. In 29 races, he finished in the top five 21 times and in the top ten 24 times.

In addition to winning the championship,

Dale also won The Winston—a NASCAR race that doesn't figure in Winston Cup points standings—and the American Driver of the Year award. The season was successful enough to push Dale's prize winnings for the year over the $2 million mark for the first time.

Dale finished third in the point standings for the 1988 season, behind crowd favorite Bill Elliott and Rusty Wallace. For just about anyone else on the Winston Cup circuit, this would have been considered a most successful campaign, but for Dale the year was a disappointment. He won only three of 29 races.

Dale was a bridesmaid rather than a bride again in 1989, finishing second for the Winston Cup championship to Rusty Wallace, who won the cup by a mere 12 points. In 29 races, Dale won five and had 14 top-five and 19 top-ten finishes. His winnings for the year were $1,435,730. Still, Dale would always remember this season as the championship that almost was.

In 1990, Earnhardt came as close to winning the Daytona 500 as he's ever come. He was leading with only half a lap left in the race when he hit some debris on the track and shredded a tire. Derrike Cope sped by and took the checkered flag.

If Earnhardt was dispirited by the loss, he did not let it get in the way of his having one of the most exciting seasons in his career.

He and Mark Martin raced neck-and-neck for the lead in the Winston Cup. Coming into the last race of the year at the Atlanta Motor Speedway, a 1.522-mile oval in Atlanta, Georgia, Dale led by a minuscule six-point margin, 4,260 to 4,254.

The difference in award money between first and second place was $670,000, so besides the considerable amount of pride on the line, there was a good deal of cash involved as well.

Earnhardt had earned his way to the top of the heap with a wild summer of spectacular victories and disappointing crashes. Even going into the Atlanta race, Dale had already set the record for most money won in a single year by a race car driver.

In addition to his Winston Cup successes, Dale had also won the International Race of Champions; and The Winston. He was already $1.5 million richer on the year, and that figure could double if he beat out Martin for the points championship.

Besides the driver championship, the

Earnhardt sticks the nose of his car inches from the tailpipe of the lead car in order to draft at the 1990 IROC race at Talladega.

A member of Bill Elliot's pit crew died in a crash at the 1990 Atlanta Journal 500.

Manufacturer's Championship was also on the line in Atlanta. The Chevrolet team—of which Dale's car was the top gun—had earned 188 points to Ford's 185.

Whereas Dale came into the race on a roll, Mark Martin's team, owned by Jack Roush, was in chaos. They had decided to change cars before the Atlanta race.

Martin tested six different Fords before the team ended up borrowing one from Davey Allison's team. The car was repainted in Martin's colors and entered in Atlanta. Right up until race time the car was a major worry, and they used every opportunity to test it and readjust it.

Dale, on the other hand, showed up at the track early in the week, ran 20 hot laps in his familiar number 3, parked it, and went bow hunting for deer for a few days.

During qualifying, Rusty Wallace ran the fastest lap, 175.222 mph, to take the pole. Dale started the race in sixth position, and Martin started in the 11th spot on the grid.

When the final practice laps were run, however, Dale was fastest with a lap at 173.060 mph, Martin was right behind him at 172.740. In the race itself, Wallace jumped out front and held the lead for the first 44 laps.

Then Dale passed him to take the lead. He didn't stay in front for long but continued to run with the lead pack, a group that included Morgan Shepherd, Bill Elliott, Darrell Waltrip, and Geoff Bodine.

Martin, on the other hand, was struggling. He stalled his car on the track, twice he had trouble getting out of pit road because of fuelfeed problems, and even when his car was running it couldn't keep up with the leaders.

Elliott moved into the lead and began to put some space between himself and the rest of the pack. Then it was time for Elliott's final scheduled pit stop of the day. Ricky Rudd tried to pull into the pit directly behind Elliott but spun and slammed backward into Elliott's car.

Mike Rich, a member of Elliott's crew, suffered massive internal injuries in the collision. Two other of Elliott's crew members were also injured. Rich was rushed to Georgia Baptist Medical Hospital where he died that night.

The race was run under somber conditions after that. Geoff Bodine led the race for a while, and then, near the end, was passed by Morgan Shepherd. On Dale's last pit stop, the wrong set of tires were put on his car and he could manage to cruise only to a third-place finish. Mark Martin finished sixth.

The difference was enough to win the Winston Cup points championship for Dale, 4,430 to 4,404.

Though Fords finished onetwo, the Chevy brought home the checkers, and that was enough to give Chevrolet the Manufacturer's Championship as well. Chevy and Ford ended the season with 194 points each but Chevy was given the championship on the grounds that its cars had won 13 races to Ford's 11.

Dale's total winnings for the year were pushed over the $3 million mark with the championship, but the quiet nature of the victory celebration reflected the tragedy of the day.

7

"I DON'T LOOK LIKE NO MILLIONAIRE"

In 1991, Dale won his fifth Winston Cup Championship. In 29 races, Dale finished in the top ten 21 times. This sounds amazing—and it is!—but it marked the sixth time in Earnhardt's career that he had over 20 finishes in the top ten.

Dale started the season with the now-expected mishap at the Daytona 500. This year he was trying to regain the lead near the end of the race when his luck ran out and he got swept up in someone else's accident.

Naturally, Dale's luck improved a lot after that. He took the checkers in the Pontiac Excitement 400, Hanes 500, DieHard 500, and the Tyson Holly Farms 400.

The DieHard win was a classic. Chevy fans call it one of the greatest races ever, as Dale in his black Chevy Lumina held off a hungry pack of Fords with pure stubbornness.

But was Dale happy with the way the season had gone? No way. In fact he was ticked off at

A top-performing pit crew is essential for any top-performing driver.

his old buddy Richard Childress. The problem was a basic difference in racing philosophy.

Dale's only real competitor in the Winston Cup point standings during the 1991 season was Ricky Rudd, who was consistent, finished races, but couldn't win one to save his life.

The fellows who were winning all of the races, namely Davey Allison and Harry Gant, had done so poorly during the first half of the season that they were no longer contenders for the points championship.

That meant that not finishing a race hurt Dale's chances to win the championship more than winning a race helped him. This led Childress to order Earnhardt to hold back.

"It was a bad year," Dale said at that year's award ceremonies in New York City. "I felt like we should have won more races. I like to go for it [the win], but I have to work with the team."

The Winston Cup championship was Dale's fifth in seven years. Did that mean he was going to kick back and take it easy for a while? No way.

"I always thought that Richard Petty's record of seven Winston Cup championships was untouchable," Dale said after winning his fifth. "But now we have five and I still think I have a few good years left in me and this team is really working together well. So seven may be reachable. And besides, I'm building a new house on my farm and there's plenty of room for a couple more Winston Cups."

Then he flashed that grin.

Dale wasn't the only one on the Richard Childress Racing/Goodwrench team who wasn't happy. Crew chief Kirk Shelmerdine saw trouble brewing. As the team became more successful,

there were more and more demands on Dale's time.

He had interviews to do, commercials to make, business meetings to attend. It all meant, Shelmerdine knew, that there was that much less time for Dale to think about racing.

In 1992, Shelmerdine's fears would turn out to be well-founded.

The 1992 Winston Cup season is the one Dale would like to forget. He didn't even finish in the top ten in the point standings come year's end, and he had won only one race.

The bad luck started, as usual, at the

Second place at the 1992 International Race of Champions was a dead heat between Hary Gant (10) and Ricky Rudd (11). The clear winner: Dale Earnhardt.

Neil Bonnett's number 31 car flips after hitting Ted Musgrave's 55 at the 1993 DieHard 500. Both drivers walked away from the crash—but Bonnett wasn't so lucky in a crash one year later.

Daytona 500. On Lap 91 of that race, during a threeway battle for the lead, Ernie Irvan tried to pass Bill Elliott and Sterling Marlin, who were running side by side at the time. Making a pass like that at Daytona is a lot like trying to thread a needle at 200 mph!

Irvin, who was the defending Daytona 500 champion, nicked Marlin as he passed. Marlin started to spin and that led to a chaotic chain reaction that ended up destroying or damaging 14 cars—including Dale's.

The irony of the crash was that Irvan would not have attempted the seemingly foolhardy pass if he hadn't seen Dale do it successfully earlier in the week during a 125-mile qualifying race.

Yes, Dale's luck in the Daytona 500 continued to be miserable. But, unlike in previous seasons, Dale's luck didn't improve much after he got out of Florida.

After seven consecutive seasons of winning more than $1 million, Dale's income slipped back into six figures. The season was bitter enough to make Dale's crew chief Kirk Shelmerdine quit the racing business completely for a while. (Shelmerdine has since returned to the business as a driver.) Replacing Kirk as Dale's crew chief was Andy Petree, who still holds that position today.

In 1993, Dale Earnhardt made another great run at the Daytona 500. On Lap 157, Dale and defending champ Al Unser, Jr., started to bump each other. Neither car was damaged, but the collision forced Unser then to bump a car driven by Bobby Hillin, Jr. Hillin lost his brakes, swerved onto the infield and then back on the track again where he was run into by Kyle Petty. Petty had been a favorite to win, along with Earnhardt, but his car didn't survive the crash.

On Lap 168, Rusty Wallace was involved in a horrible crash. Wallace had earned the nickname "Rubberhead" (as opposed to Earnhardt's nickname, "Ironhead") because of the accidents he had gotten into—and survived. Although Wallace's car disintegrated in this crash, his injuries were minor.

Dale, unbothered by these collisions, led for most of the race. On the last lap, Dale Jarrett

Earnhardt celebrates after winning the 1993 Pepsi 400.

pulled up behind Earnardt. The number 3 car had been oversteering for a while, and the draft effect of Jarrett's vehicle "got me looser," Earnhardt said later. Jarrett swung to the inside and won by 19 seconds.

"I didn't win again," Earnhardt shrugged. "What the heck."

Jarrett was more effusive. "When you beat Dale Earnhardt anywhere, anytime, you've had a day's work," he said afterwards. "He's done everything but win this race."

In 1993, Dale pulled down his sixth Winston Cup championship. He won six of 30 races, finishing in the top five in 17 of them and in the top ten in 21 of them. Dale once again broke his own record, as well as the stock car record, for most winnings in a year, with prize money totaling $3,353,789.

But the 1993 season was tainted by tragedy. On July 13, Dale lost his good buddy Davey Allison, who the previous day had crashed a helicopter he was piloting while attempting to land on the infield of the Talladega Superspeedway.

Though it was surely a coincidence, the death of Davey Allison sent Dale on a winning streak. On July 19, at the Pocono Raceway in

Long Beach, Pennsylvania, Dale's Chevy Lumina defeated Rusty Wallace's Pontiac by .72 seconds in the Miller 500.

After that victory, Dale knelt down with his crew around the number 3 car and said a prayer for Davey. Dale then drove once around the track holding a flag bearing number 28 on it.

The following Sunday, the action returned to Talladega, the scene of Allison's accident. It was a hot and muggy day, with temperatures approaching 100 degrees.

The race was as exciting as they come, with Dale defeating Ernie Irvan by about six inches. Photos of the finish had to examined by NASCAR officials before the race results were made official.

Unfortunately, once again, it was crashes and injury that stole the headlines. On Lap 70, journeyman driver Stanley Smith crashed into the unforgiving Talladega wall and suffered head injuries that had him in the hospital in critical condition. He would survive.

Then, later in the race, Dale's best buddy Neil Bonnett, driving for the first time since a near-fatal crash, had a spectacular flying accident that did such damage to the fence separating the track from the main grandstand, that the entire race had to be halted for 80 minutes while it was repaired.

Neil walked away from this accident with nothing worse than a bruised arm, but it should have been seen as a sign that he had no business being behind the wheel of a race car anymore.

Dale may have only tied Richard Petty's record for most Winston Cup championships, but he has surpassed "The King" when it comes to commercial endorsements and souvenir sales. Dale's earnings driving a race car are smallchange compared to the money he makes pushing merchandise. His own souvenir company, Dale Earnhardt, Inc., sells 749 different Earnhardt items, from T-shirts to die-cast models. In 1994, that company made about $50 million!

Nineteen ninety-four was perhaps Earnhardt's most successful year, showing that at age 42 he wasn't getting older, he was getting stronger. In 31 races, he had 25 top ten finishes, the most in his 20 years of Winston Cup racing. Four of those 25 top-ten finishes were victories, and Earnhardt not only claimed his seventh driving championship—tying him with the great Richard Petty—but he also won $3,400,733 in prize money. It was the third time he had won over three million dollars in prize money, and the greatest amount he had ever earned.

In 1995, the Richard Childress Racing/Goodwrench car is still black and it still has a big white 3 on the side, but now it's a Monte Carlo instead of a Lumina. The Chevrolet Monte Carlo returned to NASCAR, after being gone for five years.

It is one slick-looking car. The Monte Carlo has more graceful lines than the Lumina, with a slender rounded nose that looks flat out fast. The Monte Carlo is cutting-edge aerodynamics.

And it isn't just the stock-car version that looks that way, either. Dale's car is firmly based on the production model.

Don Taylor, NASCAR Program Manager for the General Motors Motorsports Technology

Group; says, "The differences between the race and street versions are really very subtle.

"The hood, roof, decklid, windshield and backlight are all production—although Lexan is used instead of glass for safety. The race car's silhouette is the same as a Monte Carlo in a dealership showroom."

To cut down on his busy schedule, and to allow him to better focus his attentions on Winston Cup racing, Dale retired from the Busch Grand National racing circuit after the 1994 season.

No more two-race weekends. From now on, he will only race on Sunday—and when he's not racing, you can find him on his 300-acre chicken farm in Mooresville, North Carolina, about 40 miles north of Charlotte. Even if you can't find him, he's still probably there. His wife, Teresa, and his kids have learned to stop worrying.

"I can go out on the farm at daylight," Dale says, "and not come back until dark and she [Teresa] wonders what I've been doing all day."

Have the riches of his success changed Dale Earnhardt? Everyone, including Dale, seems to think not.

Dale says, "You should see me at home on the farm. I don't look like no millionaire. I got a '72 dump truck, rusty ol' claptrap thing. I drive it setting way up there with a big ol' gearshift sticking up by my ear. I come tearin' around a turn over a hill, it's blowing smoke, I'm sideways, sticks and limbs are hanging out the side and branches are flying out the back, and you better get out of the way, because that'll be me, and I don't back off for no one!"

That's Dale, all right.

What does Dale plan to do with himself

when he retires as an active driver? That's an easy one. He never plans on straying too far from the race track.

Although Dale would not consider owning a racing team while he is still an active driver, but once retired, he says, "If I do want a team, it's going to be in the way that I can enjoy it. That means I'd have to find a young driver I want to set the world on fire with."

Someone like himself, he means.

STATISTICS

DALE EARNHARDT

YEAR	RACES	WINS	TOP 5	TOP 10	TOTAL $ WON
1975	1	0	0	0	$1,925
1976	2	0	0	0	3,085
1977	1	0	0	0	1,375
1978	5	0	1	2	20,145
1979	27	1	11	17	264,086
1980	31	5	19	24	588,926*
1981	31	0	9	17	347,113
1982	30	1	7	17	375,325
1983	30	2	9	14	446,272
1984	30	2	12	22	616,788
1985	28	4	10	16	546,596
1986	29	5	16	23	1,768,880*
1987	29	11	21	24	2,069,243*
1988	29	3	13	19	1,214,089
1989	29	5	14	19	1,435,730
1990	29	9	18	23	3,083,056*
1991	29	4	14	21	2,396,685*
1992	29	1	6	15	863,885
1993	30	6	17	21	3,353,789*
1994	31	4	20	25	3,400,733*
CAREER	480	63	217	314	$22,797,726

*won Winston Cup championship.

CHRONOLOGY

1952   Dale is born April 29, in Kannapolis, North Carolina.

1956   Dale's father, Ralph, wins the NASCAR Sportsman championship.

1975   Dale makes his first Winston Cup start in the World 600.

1978   Dale becomes a star with a second-place finish in the World Service Life 300 at Charlotte, after a race-long duel with the legendary Bobby Allison.

1979   Dale is named the Winston Cup Rookie of the Year.

1980   Dale's wins his first Winston Cup championship.

1986   In the final race of the year, the Atlanta Journal 500, Dale not only wins the race and clinches his second Winston Cup championship, but he shatters the track speed record in the process.

1987   Dale wins 11 Winston Cup races, a personal best for him, and brings home his third Winston Cup championship.

1990   Dale squeaks past Mark Martin to winthe Winston Cup championship—his fourth.

1991   Dale wins his fifth Winston Cup championship. In 29 races, Dale finishes in the top ten an amazing 21 times!

1993   Dale wins sixth Winston Cup championship.

1994   Dale's eventh Winston Cup championship ties him with the great Richard Petty.

SUGGESTIONS FOR FURTHER READING

Benson, Michael, ed., *Stock Car Spectacular*, Avenel, New Jersey: Crescent Books, 1995.

Cockerham, Paul W., *The Great Drivers*, New York: Starlog Telecommunications, 1994.

Cockerham, Paul W., *NASCAR's Greatest Races*, New York: Starlog Telecommunications, 1994.

Golenbock, Peter, *American Zoom*, New York: Macmillan Publishing Company, 1993.

ABOUT THE AUTHOR

Michael Benson is the editor of *Stock Car Spectacular* magazine. His previous books include *Vintage Science Fiction Films, Ballparks of North America, Dream Teams, Who's Who in the JFK Assassination, Monster Trucks*, and *Pickup Trucks*. He is also the editor of *Super Trucks, Monster Truck Spectacular, Military Technical Journal*, and *All Time Baseball Greats* magazines. A graduate of Hofstra University, Benson lives in Brooklyn, New York, with his wife and daughter.

INDEX

PICTURE CREDITS
Reuters/Bettmann: 2; c International Speedway Corporation/NASCAR: 8, 10, 13, 16, 26, 45, 47, 48, 50; AP/Wide World Photos: 20, 38, 44, 50, 53, 54, 56; Bruce Craig Photos, Phillipsburg, NJ: 22, 34; UPI/Bettmann: 42.